Grandpa's Soup

Written by Eiko Kadono
Illustrated by Satomi Ichikawa

EERDMANS BOOKS FOR YOUNG READERS
GRAND RAPIDS, MICHIGAN / CAMBRIDGE, U. K.

After Grandma died, Grandpa was all alone. He felt too sad to do anything. Every day he would drink the milk that the milkman brought to his house, eat the bread that he bought at the store, and then just sit by himself. Every day, day after day, was the same.

Then one day, Grandpa woke up and said to himself, "I want to eat hot soup. I want to eat again the meatball soup that my dear wife used to make for me."

Grandpa had five pots in his kitchen, all lined up on a shelf from biggest to smallest. "Maybe I can make the meatball soup myself. Since it will just be for me, this little pan will be big enough," Grandpa said, reaching for the smallest pot.

"My wife used to sing when she made this soup," he remembered.

> " 'Boil the water.
> Roll the meatballs round.
> Drop them in the water — plop.
> Add a little salt and pepper.
> Add a little butter.'

That's what she used to sing."

So Grandpa went to the market and bought ground meat and cooked his first batch of soup.

"Ah, my meatball soup is done." Just as Grandpa said that, he heard small footsteps outside his door. *Tip, tip, tip.* When Grandpa opened the door, there stood three mice.

"Hm, it smells so good!" they said, their three little noses twitching with excitement.

Grandpa poured soup into three little saucers for the mice. *Sip, sip, sip.* The mice licked the saucers clean. "Thank you!" they said and went home.

Only a little bit of soup was left in the pot. Grandpa put it in his bowl and ate it. Then tipping his head to one side he said, "My wife's soup tasted much better than this. I wonder why."

The next day, Grandpa took the second smallest pot from the shelf.

"Even if the mice come again, this pot will hold enough for them and for me. Now what did my wife sing again?

    'Boil the water.
    Roll the meatballs round.
    Drop them in the water — plop.'

Then, oh, yes, she would sing,

    'Add some small potatoes
    after taking off their skin.
    Add a little salt and pepper.
    Add a little butter.'

I used to love to hear her sing like that."

So Grandpa went to the market for ground meat and some small potatoes and then went home and cooked the soup.

"Oh, good. My soup is done," said Grandpa. Just then he heard small footsteps outside his door. *Tip, tip, tip, thip.* He opened the door and found the three mice from yesterday and a cat.

"Hmm," they said. "It smells so good!"

"Oh, my!" said Grandpa. "What a surprise to see mice and a cat come together!"

"When we have good food," said the mice and cat, "we are good friends."

"I see," said Grandpa. "So I guess you want to eat together." Grandpa put soup into three saucers and a small bowl. Three saucers for the mice and a small bowl for the cat.

Sip, sip, sip, lap. The mice and cat finished their soup, said "Thank you," and went home.

"Again today, there is only a little bit of soup left in the pot. I should have cooked more," said Grandpa. Grandpa put the rest of the soup into his bowl and ate it. Then he tipped his head to one side and sighed, "My wife's soup tasted much better than this. I wonder why."

The next day, Grandpa took the third smallest pot from his shelf.

"Even if the mice and the cat come again, this pot should be large enough and there will be some soup left for me, too. Now, my dear wife used to sing,

> 'Boil the water.
> Roll the meatballs round.
> Drop them in the water — plop.
> Add some small potatoes
> after taking off their skin.'

Then . . . I'm remembering now,

> 'Chop some tiny onions.
> Drop them in.
> Add a little salt and pepper.
> Add a little butter.'"

So Grandpa went to the market, bought ground meat, small potatoes, and tiny onions, and started cooking the soup.

"Now my meatball soup is ready," said Grandpa just as he heard small footsteps again outside his door. *Tip, tip, tip, thip, click.* Opening the door he found the mice, the cat, and a dog standing there.

"Hmmm, that smells so good," they said.

"Oh, I see that you are all good friends," said Grandpa. So Grandpa poured soup for all of them. Three saucers for the mice, a small bowl for the cat, a medium-sized bowl for the dog.

Sip, sip, sip, lap, gulp. The mice, the cat, and the dog ate their soup, said "Thank you," and went away.

This day, again, only a little bit of soup was left in the pan. Grandpa poured it into his bowl, ate it, and said, "I should have cooked more." Then, tipping his head, he said, "My dear wife's soup was much better than this. I wonder why."

The next day, Grandpa took his biggest pan, not even bothering with the fourth biggest, off the shelf. "This has to be big enough. Even if the mice, the cat, the dog, and someone else come, there will be some left for me. Now, let me remember again what my wife used to sing.

> 'Boil the water.
> Roll the meatballs round.
> Drop them in the water — plop.
> Add some small potatoes
> after taking off their skin.
> Chop some tiny onions.
> Drop them in.'

Oh, yes! She would sing about carrots, too.

> 'Slice some carrots nice and thin.
> Add a little salt and pepper.
> Add a little butter.'"

Grandpa went to the market for ground meat, small potatoes, tiny onions, and thin carrots. Then he started cooking.

"Well, the meatball soup is ready," said Grandpa. Again he heard footsteps outside his door. *Tip, tip, tip, thip, click, clomp.*

Opening the door, Grandpa found the mice, the cat, the dog, and a boy standing there.

"Hmmmm, that smells so good!" they said

"So," said Grandpa. "You are all good friends today, too. Let me treat you to some soup."

"Is that all right? Is it really all right?" asked the boy with a delighted smile.

"Of course," said Grandpa, beaming. "I cooked meatball soup in such a large pot that there is enough for everyone. Please come in and eat as much as you like."

Then the boy turned around and shouted, "Come on everyone! Stop hiding! The Grandpa is going to treat us to soup!"

Clomp, clomp, clomp, clomp, clompclompclompclompclomp . . .
1, 2, 3, 4, 5, 6, 7, 8, 9 more children came running into the
house.

"Well, well," said Grandpa, a little surprised. But right away,
he counted them all again — just to be sure — and took out
saucers and bowls for everyone. Three saucers for the mice, a
little bowl for the cat, a medium-sized bowl for the dog, and
ten big bowls for the children. Then he poured out soup for
each of them.

*Sip, sip sip, lap, gulp, slurp, slurp, slurp, slurp, slurpslurpslurp-
slurpslurpslurp . . .*

"Grandpa, why don't you eat with us?" asked the children.

Grandpa looked into the pot and saw that, again today, only a little bit of soup was left.

"Okay," said Grandpa. "Let's all eat together." And Grandpa poured the last of the soup into his bowl and ate.

"It's good! It's delicious!" said Grandpa. "Finally, it tastes just like the soup my dear wife used to make!"

Then, with a smile, he said, "Tomorrow I will cook the soup using ALL of my pots!"

Text copyright © 1997 Eiko Kadono
Illustrations copyright © 1997 Satomi Ichikawa

First published in 1997 in Japanese under the title "ODANGO SUPU"
Published by Kaisei-Sha Publishing Co., Ltd.
English translation rights arranged with Kaisei-Sha Publishing Co., Ltd. through Japan Foreign-Rights Centre
All rights reserved

This edition published in 1999 in the United States by
Eerdmans Books for Young Readers
An imprint of Wm. B. Eerdmans Publishing Company
255 Jefferson Ave. S.E., Grand Rapids, Michigan 49503/
P.O. Box 163, Cambridge CB3 9PU U.K.

Printed and bound in Singapore

05 04 03 02 01 00 99   7 6 5 4 3 2 1

Library of Congress cataloging-in-publication data
Kadono, Eiko.
Grandpa's Soup / written by Eiko Kadono ; illustrated by Satomi Ichikawa.
p. cm.
Summary: After the death of his wife, an old man gradually realizes that making the soup she used to cook and sharing it with friends eases his loneliness.
ISBN 0-8028-5195-9 (cloth : alk. paper)
(1. Soups Fiction. 2. Loneliness Fiction. 3. Grief Fiction. 4. Sharing Fiction.) I. Ichikawa, Satomi. ill. II. Title.
PZ7.K1167Gr 1999
(E)—dc21   99-30712
                         CIP